contents

Australian spoon and cup measurements are metric. A conversion chart appears on page 62.

GRILLS &

An essential part of the great Aussie get-together, the grill and the barbecue are versatile, healthy and easy ways to cook. Of course, there's the unique flavour, aroma and those great char-grill marks, too. Seafood, meat and poultry, vegies, fruit and even bread all taste fantastic when infused with the smoky flavour of char-grilling. Just before heating, brush or spray both food and barbecue, grill pan or grill with melted butter or oil (aerosol sprays aren't suitable on all cookware surfaces – check manufacturer's instructions). A closed or kettle barbecue can be used to cook food with either direct or indirect heat.

To cook on direct heat, place food directly over the heat source. For indirect heat, set food in the middle of the barbecue and move the heat source to the outside edges. Indirect cooking is best for roasting large pieces of meat. Cook food for a few minutes without moving it so char-grill marks will be clearly defined. Turn food once only and baste frequently with butter, oil or marinade while it is cooking. To avoid scorched or dry food, large or thick items can be finished off in a moderate oven. Remember to remove seafood when it is still a little underdone – its own heat will finish cooking it by the time it is served.

BARBECUES

New barbecues and grill pans need be seasoned before use. This will enhance the flavour of the food, and create a smooth surface that food is less likely to stick to. Season barbecues or grill pans by following manufacturer's instructions or by wiping with a paper towel dipped in a cooking oil such as peanut oil (not a polyunsaturated oil, which tends to make the surface sticky), and heat on high for 1 hour. Let it cool and repeat several times. Care for them by washing immediately with very hot water, and use a sponge or stiff brush; dry thoroughly. Spray the metal parts of your barbecue with oil and wipe off surplus before covering. Cooking food under the grill produces a lovely browned surface on everything from sausages to an omelette. Grilling is also healthy as excess fat ends up in the pan under the rack, ready to discard. Always preheat the griller on high before cooking so food starts to brown immediately. The time to heat your grill will depend on the make of grill you have, but an approximate guide is 5 to 10 minutes. Brush or spray the food and the tray with melted butter or cooking-oil spray just before cooking. Soak to loosen "cooked on" bits or, to avoid cleaning altogether, you can cover the entire pan with heavy foil or use disposable aluminium griller trays, available from supermarkets.

herbed blue-eye skewers
with potato smash and skordalia

*Skordalia is a classic Greek
accompaniment for grilled
meats or seafood.*

800g blue-eye fillets, cut
   into 2cm pieces
¼ cup (60ml) olive oil
2 tablespoons finely chopped
   fresh flat-leaf parsley
2 tablespoons finely chopped
   fresh lemon thyme
1kg baby new potatoes,
   unpeeled
½ cup (120g) sour cream
40g butter, softened
skordalia
1 small potato (120g)
1 slice white bread
2 cloves garlic, crushed
1 tablespoon cider vinegar
¼ cup (60ml) water
2 tablespoons olive oil

1 Thread fish onto eight skewers; place in
medium shallow dish. Brush with combined
oil and herbs. Cover; refrigerate 20 minutes.
2 Meanwhile, make skordalia.
3 Boil, steam or microwave potatoes until
tender; drain. Mash half the potatoes in medium
bowl with sour cream and butter until smooth.
Using fork, crush remaining potatoes until
skins burst; fold into mash mixture. Cover to
keep warm.
4 Cook skewers on heated oiled grill plate
(or grill or barbecue). Serve fish skewers with
skordalia and potato smash.
skordalia Boil, steam or microwave potato
until tender; drain. Mash potato in medium
bowl until smooth. Discard crusts from bread.
Soak bread in small bowl of cold water; drain.
Squeeze out excess water. Blend or process
bread with remaining ingredients until smooth.
Stir bread mixture into potato.

serves 4
preparation time 20 minutes
(plus refrigeration time)
cooking time 30 minutes
nutritional count per serving 44.7g total fat
(16.7g saturated fat); 3114kJ (745 cal);
39.8g carbohydrate; 42.9g protein; 5.3g fibre
tip You need to soak eight bamboo skewers in
cold water before using to prevent them from
splintering and scorching during cooking.

seared salmon kerala-style with lime pickle yogurt

2 teaspoons coriander seeds
1 teaspoon cumin seeds
2 cardamom pods, bruised
1 cinnamon stick
1 teaspoon ground turmeric
½ teaspoon chilli powder
2 tablespoons peanut oil
2 cloves garlic, crushed
4 x 265g salmon cutlets
100g baby spinach leaves
lime pickle yogurt
½ cup (140g) yogurt
2 tablespoons lime pickle, chopped finely

1   Dry-fry coriander, cumin, cardamom and cinnamon in small heated frying pan, stirring, over medium heat until fragrant. Stir in turmeric and chilli powder; remove from heat.
2   Using mortar and pestle, crush spices until ground finely; transfer to large bowl. Stir in oil and garlic, add fish; turn fish to coat in marinade. Cover; refrigerate 30 minutes.
3   Meanwhile, make lime pickle yogurt.
4   Cook fish on heated oiled grill plate (or grill or barbecue). Serve fish with spinach and yogurt.
lime pickle   Combine ingredients in small bowl.

serves 4
preparation time 20 minutes (plus refrigeration time)
cooking time 15 minutes
nutritional count per serving 29.3g total fat (6.7g saturated fat); 2082kJ (498 cal); 3.9g carbohydrate; 54.1g protein; 1.1g fibre
tip Lime pickle is an Indian mixed pickle condiment of limes that adds a hot and spicy taste to meals. Available from Indian food stores.

grilled snapper fillets with fennel and onion salad

1 medium red onion (170g), sliced thinly
4 green onions, sliced thinly
1 large fennel bulb (550g), trimmed, sliced thinly
2 trimmed celery stalks (200g), sliced thinly
½ cup coarsely chopped fresh flat-leaf parsley
⅓ cup (80ml) orange juice
¼ cup (60ml) olive oil
2 cloves garlic, crushed
2 teaspoons sambal oelek
4 x 275g snapper fillets, skin on

1   Combine onions, fennel, celery and parsley in medium bowl.
2   Place juice, oil, garlic and sambal in screw-top jar; shake well.
3   Cook fish on heated oiled grill plate (or grill or barbecue) until browned both sides and cooked as desired.
4   Pour half the dressing over salad in bowl; toss gently to combine. Serve salad topped with fish; drizzle with remaining dressing.

serves 4
preparation time 15 minutes
cooking time 10 minutes
nutritional count per serving 20g total fat (3.9g saturated fat); 1898kJ (454 cal); 7g carbohydrate; 58.3g protein; 4.5g fibre

char-grilled bream and vegetables with chilli basil butter sauce

4 baby cauliflowers (500g), halved
2 trimmed corn cobs (500g), cut into 2cm rounds
400g baby carrots, trimmed
2 tablespoons olive oil
4 x 240g whole bream
chilli basil butter sauce
80g butter
2 fresh small red thai chillies, chopped finely
⅓ cup firmly packed fresh basil leaves, shredded finely
1 tablespoon lemon juice

1 Place vegetables and half the oil in large bowl; toss to combine. Cook vegetables on heated oiled grill plate (or grill or barbecue) about 20 minutes or until browned all over and cooked through.
2 Meanwhile, make chilli basil butter sauce.
3 Score each fish three times both sides; brush all over with remaining oil. Cook fish on heated oiled grill plate (or grill or barbecue) about 5 minutes each side or until cooked as desired. Serve fish and vegetables drizzled with sauce.
chilli basil butter sauce Melt butter in small saucepan; add chilli, basil and juice, stir until combined.

serves 4
preparation time 20 minutes
cooking time 30 minutes
nutritional count per serving 32.2g total fat (13.9g saturated fat); 2608kJ (624 cal); 22.7g carbohydrate; 56.4g protein; 9.3g fibre
tip Substitute bream fillets for whole bream, if desired.

11

black bean and chilli prawn kebabs

1kg uncooked medium prawns
½ cup (125ml) japanese soy sauce
1½ tablespoons salted black beans, rinsed, chopped coarsely
1 clove garlic, crushed
2cm piece fresh ginger (10g), grated
1 tablespoon dry sherry
1 teaspoon sesame oil
1 fresh small red thai chilli, chopped finely
1 fresh small red thai chilli, sliced thinly

1 Shell and devein prawns.
2 Combine 2 tablespoons of the sauce with beans, garlic, ginger, sherry, oil and chopped chilli in large bowl; add prawns. Cover; refrigerate 3 hours or overnight.
3 Drain prawns; discard marinade. Thread prawns onto 12 skewers.
4 Cook prawns on heated oiled grill plate (or grill or barbecue) until browned both sides.
5 Serve prawns with combined remaining sauce and sliced chilli.

serves 4
preparation time 30 minutes (plus refrigeration time)
cooking time 10 minutes
nutritional count per serving 2.8 total fat (0.4g saturated fat); 836kJ (200 cal); 4g carbohydrate; 37.2g protein; 0.4g fibre
tip If using bamboo skewers, soak them in water for at least an hour before using, to avoid splintering and scorching during cooking.

char-grilled scallop and witlof salad with orange gremolata

2 red witlof (250g), quartered
16 scallops (400g), roe removed
orange dressing
2 tablespoons olive oil
1 tablespoon orange juice
orange gremolata
¼ cup finely chopped fresh flat-leaf parsley
1 tablespoon finely grated orange rind
1 clove garlic, crushed

1 Make orange dressing. Make orange gremolata.
2 Cook witlof on heated oiled grill plate (or grill or barbecue)
until browned lightly.
3 Cook scallops on grill plate until cooked.
4 Drizzle witlof and scallops with dressing and serve accompanied
with gremolata.
orange dressing Combine ingredients in small jug.
orange gremolata Combine ingredients in small bowl.

serves 4
preparation time 10 minutes
cooking time 10 minutes
nutritional count per serving 9.9g total fat (1.5g saturated fat);
615kJ (147 cal); 1.7g carbohydrate; 12.3g protein; 1.4g fibre

chicken wings and green mango salad

10cm stick fresh lemon grass
(20g), chopped finely
1 long green chilli,
chopped finely
3 cloves garlic, crushed
10 fresh kaffir lime leaves,
shredded finely
16 chicken wings (1.5kg)
2 small green mangoes (600g)
1 large carrot (180g)
1 lebanese cucumber (130g)
1 medium red capsicum (200g),
sliced thinly
2 green onions, sliced thinly
sweet and sour dressing
2 tablespoons fish sauce
2 tablespoons lime juice
2 tablespoons grated
palm sugar
1 tablespoon white vinegar
1 tablespoon water

1 Make sweet and sour dressing.

2 Combine lemon grass, chilli, garlic, half the lime leaves and 2 tablespoons of the dressing in medium bowl, add chicken; toss chicken to coat in marinade. Cover chicken and remaining dressing separately; refrigerate overnight.

3 Drain chicken; discard marinade. Cook chicken on heated oiled grill plate (or grill or barbecue), uncovered, until cooked through.

4 Meanwhile, use vegetable peeler to finely slice mangoes, carrot and cucumber into ribbons. Place in medium bowl with capsicum, remaining lime leaves and remaining dressing; toss gently to combine. Serve chicken with salad, sprinkled with onion.

sweet and sour dressing Place ingredients in screw-top jar; shake well.

serves 4
preparation time 20 minutes
(plus refrigeration time)
cooking time 15 minutes
nutritional count per serving 13g total fat
(4.1g saturated fat); 1919kJ (459 cal);
25.3g carbohydrate; 57.4g protein; 4.3g fibre

grilled thigh fillets
with salsa verde and kipfler smash

8 chicken thigh fillets (880g)
600g kipfler potatoes, unpeeled
50g butter, chopped
salsa verde
½ cup coarsely chopped fresh flat-leaf parsley
¼ cup coarsely chopped fresh mint
⅓ cup (80ml) olive oil
½ cup (125ml) lemon juice
¼ cup (50g) rinsed, drained capers, chopped coarsely
8 anchovy fillets, drained, chopped finely
2 cloves garlic, crushed

1 Make salsa verde.
2 Place ⅓ cup of the salsa verde in medium bowl; add chicken, turn to coat in salsa marinade.
3 Cook chicken on heated oiled grill plate (or grill or barbecue) until browned both sides and cooked through.
4 Meanwhile, boil, steam or microwave potatoes until tender; drain. Using potato masher, crush potato roughly in large bowl with butter.
5 Serve chicken, topped with remaining salsa verde and potato.
salsa verde Combine ingredients in small bowl.

serves 4
preparation time 15 minutes
cooking time 25 minutes
nutritional count per serving 45.3g total fat (14.3g saturated fat); 2897kJ (693 cal); 22.1g carbohydrate; 47.2g protein; 3.5g fibre

piri piri chicken thigh fillets

4 fresh long red chillies, chopped coarsely
1 teaspoon dried chilli flakes
2 cloves garlic, quartered
1 teaspoon sea salt
2 tablespoons olive oil
1 tablespoon cider vinegar
2 teaspoons brown sugar
8 x 125g chicken thigh fillets

1 Using mortar and pestle, grind fresh chilli, chilli flakes, garlic and salt to make piri piri paste.
2 Combine paste with oil, vinegar, sugar and chicken in medium bowl. Cook chicken on heated oiled grill plate (or grill or barbecue) until cooked through. Serve with lime wedges, if desired.

serves 4
preparation time 10 minutes
cooking time 15 minutes
nutritional count per serving 27.2g total fat (6.8g saturated fat); 1822kJ (436 cal); 1.8g carbohydrate; 46.6g protein; 0.3g fibre

steak sandwich with tarragon and tomato salsa

4 x 125g scotch fillet steaks
2 cloves garlic, crushed
1 tablespoon dijon mustard
1 tablespoon olive oil
8 thick slices bread (360g)
⅓ cup (100g) mayonnaise
40g trimmed watercress

tarragon and tomato salsa
2 cloves garlic, crushed
3 large egg tomatoes (270g),
   quartered, sliced thinly
½ small red onion (50g),
   sliced thinly
1 tablespoon finely chopped
   fresh tarragon

1 Combine beef, garlic, mustard and half the oil in medium bowl.
2 Make tarragon and tomato salsa.
3 Cook beef on heated grill plate (or grill or barbecue) until cooked as desired. Remove from heat, cover; stand 5 minutes.
4 Meanwhile, brush both sides of bread with remaining oil; toast on same grill. Spread one side of each slice with mayonnaise; sandwich watercress, beef and salsa between slices.
tarragon and tomato salsa Combine ingredients in medium bowl.

serves 4
preparation time 15 minutes
cooking time 15 minutes
nutritional count per serving 21.6g total fat (4.6g saturated fat); 2161kJ (517 cal); 43.3g carbohydrate; 35g protein; 4.2g fibre
tips Use ciabatta, focaccia or even individual pide (turkish bread) for this recipe.
You need 80g watercress to get the amount of trimmed watercress required for this recipe.

beef burger with grilled eggplant and rocket

⅓ cup (95g) greek-style yogurt
⅓ cup (90g) hummus
1 medium eggplant (300g)
500g beef mince
2 cloves garlic, crushed
1 tablespoon tomato paste
1 small brown onion (80g),
    chopped finely
1 fresh small red thai chilli,
    chopped finely
½ cup coarsely chopped
    fresh basil
½ cup (35g) stale
    breadcrumbs
1 egg
1 loaf turkish bread (430g),
    cut into quarters
40g baby rocket leaves

1 Combine yogurt and hummus in small bowl.
2 Cut eggplant into 6 slices lengthways; discard two skin-side pieces.
3 Combine beef, garlic, paste, onion, chilli, basil, breadcrumbs and egg in large bowl; shape mixture into four patties. Cook patties and eggplant, in batches, on heated oiled flat plate (or grill or barbecue) until browned both sides and cooked through.
4 Preheat grill.
5 Halve bread pieces horizontally; toast, cut-sides up. Spread cut-sides with yogurt mixture; sandwich eggplant, patties and rocket between toast pieces.

serves 4
preparation time 20 minutes
cooking time 15 minutes
nutritional count per serving 19.3g total fat (6.4g saturated fat); 2546kJ (609 cal); 61.8g carbohydrate; 42.6g protein; 7.5g fibre

sweet chilli beef ribs

½ cup (125ml) sweet chilli sauce
1 tablespoon japanese soy sauce
¼ cup (60ml) rice wine
2 cloves garlic, crushed
1cm piece fresh ginger (5cm), grated
2 tablespoons finely chopped fresh coriander
1.5kg beef spare ribs

1 Combine ingredients in large shallow dish. Cover; refrigerate 3 hours or overnight.
2 Cook ribs in covered barbecue, using indirect heat, following manufacturer's instructions, about 30 minutes or until browned all over and cooked as desired.

serves 4
preparation time 10 minutes (plus refrigeration time)
cooking time 30 minutes
nutritional count per serving 17g total fat (7g saturated fat); 1814kJ (434 cal); 7.2g carbohydrate; 58.8g protein; 1.8g fibre

spicy beef and bean salad

¼ cup (60ml) olive oil
35g packet taco seasoning mix
600g piece beef eye fillet
2 tablespoons lime juice
1 clove garlic, crushed
420g can four-bean mix, rinsed, drained
310g can corn kernels, rinsed, drained
2 lebanese cucumbers (260g), chopped finely
1 small red onion (100g), chopped finely
1 large red capsicum (350g), chopped finely
½ cup coarsely chopped fresh coriander
1 fresh long red chilli, chopped finely

1 Combine 1 tablespoon of the oil, seasoning and beef in medium bowl. Cook beef on heated grill plate (or grill or barbecue) until cooked as desired. Cover, stand 5 minutes then slice thinly.
2 Meanwhile, whisk remaining oil, juice and garlic in large bowl. Add remaining ingredients; toss gently to combine. Serve beef with salad; sprinkle with coriander leaves, if desired.

serves 4
preparation time 10 minutes
cooking time 20 minutes
nutritional count per serving 22.2g total fat (5.2g saturated fat); 2111kJ (505 cal); 30.9g carbohydrate; 40.4g protein; 9.3g fibre

chilli and honey barbecued steak with coleslaw

2 tablespoons barbecue sauce
1 tablespoon worcestershire sauce
1 tablespoon honey
1 fresh long red chilli, chopped finely
1 clove garlic, crushed
4 x 200g beef new-york cut steaks
coleslaw
2 tablespoons mayonnaise
1 tablespoon white wine vinegar
2 cups (160g) finely shredded white cabbage
1 cup (160g) finely shredded red cabbage
1 medium carrot (120g), grated coarsely
3 thinly sliced green onions

1 Combine sauces, honey, chilli and garlic in large bowl; add beef, turn to coat in honey mixture.
2 Meanwhile, make coleslaw.
3 Cook beef on heated oiled grill plate (or grill or barbecue) until browned both sides and cooked as desired.
4 Serve steaks with coleslaw.
coleslaw Place mayonnaise and vinegar in screw-top jar; shake well. Place dressing in large bowl with cabbages, carrot and onions; toss to combine.

serves 4
preparation time 15 minutes
cooking time 10 minutes
nutritional count per serving 15.2g total fat (5.4g saturated fat); 1605kJ (383 cal); 16.6g carbohydrate; 44g protein; 3.6g fibre

31

veal cutlets with green olive salsa and barbecued kipflers

2 tablespoons olive oil
2 cloves garlic, crushed
1 tablespoon finely chopped
  fresh oregano
2 teaspoons finely grated
  lemon rind
1 tablespoon lemon juice
4 x 125g veal cutlets
green olive salsa
1 tablespoon lemon juice
¼ cup coarsely chopped fresh
  flat-leaf parsley
½ cup (80g) finely chopped
  large green olives
1 small green capsicum
  (150g), chopped finely
1 tablespoon olive oil
1 clove garlic, crushed
1 tablespoon finely chopped
  fresh oregano
barbecued kipflers
1.5kg kipfler potatoes
¼ cup fresh thyme leaves
1 tablespoon coarsely grated
  lemon rind
2 cloves crushed garlic
⅓ cup (80ml) olive oil
¼ cup (60ml) lemon juice

1 Make green olive salsa; make barbecued kipflers.
2 Combine oil, garlic, oregano, rind and juice in small bowl; brush mixture over veal. Cook veal on heated oiled grill plate (or grill or barbecue) until browned both sides and cooked as desired.
3 Serve veal with salsa and potatoes.
green olive salsa Combine ingredients in small bowl.
barbecued kipflers Boil, steam or microwave potatoes until tender; drain. Halve potatoes lengthways. Combine thyme, rind, garlic, oil, juice and potato in large bowl; toss to coat in mixture. Cook potato on heated oiled grill plate (or grill or barbecue) about 15 minutes or until browned.

serves 4
preparation time 20 minutes
cooking time 30 minutes
nutritional count per serving 35g total fat (5.3g saturated fat); 2897kJ (692 cal); 55.9g carbohydrate; 32.6g protein; 9.1g fibre

fennel-flavoured veal chops with garlic mustard butter

2 teaspoons fennel seeds
1 teaspoon sea salt
½ teaspoon cracked black pepper
2 tablespoons olive oil
4 x 200g veal chops
4 flat mushrooms (320g)
80g baby rocket leaves
garlic mustard butter
80g butter, softened
1 tablespoon coarsely chopped fresh flat-leaf parsley
1 clove garlic, crushed
1 tablespoon wholegrain mustard

1 Using mortar and pestle, crush combined seeds, salt and pepper coarsely; stir in oil. Rub mixture all over veal.
2 Cook veal and mushrooms on heated oiled grill plate (or grill or barbecue) until browned both sides and cooked as desired.
3 Meanwhile, make garlic mustard butter.
4 Divide rocket among plates; top each with mushroom, veal then butter.
garlic mustard butter Combine ingredients in small bowl.

serves 4
preparation time 10 minutes
cooking time 15 minutes
nutritional count per serving 29.7g total fat (13.2g saturated fat); 1831kJ (438 cal); 2.1g carbohydrate; 39.9g protein; 2.7g fibre

za'atar-crusted kebabs with hummus

*Za'atar is a Middle-Eastern
blend of roasted dried spices;
you can make your own, as
shown here, or you can
purchase it ready-made from
Middle-Eastern food stores.*

1 tablespoon olive oil
1 tablespoon lemon juice
800g diced lamb
8 pieces lavash bread
½ cup coarsely chopped fresh
   flat-leaf parsley
200g yogurt
hummus
2 x 300g cans chickpeas,
   rinsed, drained
1 clove garlic, quartered
½ cup (140g) tahini
½ cup (125ml) lemon juice
½ cup (125ml) water
za'atar
1 tablespoon sumac
1 tablespoon toasted
   sesame seeds
1 teaspoon dried marjoram
2 teaspoons dried thyme

1 Make hummus. Make za'atar.
2 Combine oil and juice in medium bowl;
add lamb, toss to coat in mixture. Thread
lamb onto eight skewers.
3 Spread za'atar on tray. Roll kebabs in
za'atar until coated all over. Cook kebabs on
heated oiled grill plate (or grill or barbecue),
uncovered, until cooked as desired.
4 Spread hummus over lavash; top with
kebabs, sprinkle with parsley. Serve with yogurt.
hummus Blend or process ingredients until
smooth. Cover; refrigerate until required.
za'atar Combine ingredients in small bowl.

serves 4
preparation time 20 minutes
cooking time 15 minutes
nutritional count per serving 51.6g total fat
(13.3g saturated fat); 4761kJ (1136 cal);
89.9g carbohydrate; 70.9g protein; 14.5g fibre
tip If using bamboo skewers, soak them in
water for at least an hour before using, to avoid
splintering and scorching during cooking.

teriyaki lamb with carrot salad

2 tablespoons japanese soy sauce
2 tablespoons mirin
1 teaspoon caster sugar
600g diced lamb
9 green onions
carrot salad
2 medium carrots (240g), cut into matchsticks
1 cup (80g) bean sprouts
1 small red onion (100g), sliced thinly
1 tablespoon toasted sesame seeds
2 teaspoons japanese soy sauce
1 tablespoon mirin
½ teaspoon white sugar
2 teaspoons peanut oil

1 Combine sauce, mirin, sugar and lamb in medium bowl.
2 Cut four 3cm-long pieces from trimmed root end of each onion.
3 Thread lamb and onion pieces, alternately, on 12 skewers; cook on heated oiled grill plate (or grill or barbecue), brushing with soy mixture occasionally, until lamb is cooked as desired.
4 Meanwhile, make carrot salad. Serve teriyaki lamb with salad.
carrot salad Combine carrot, sprouts, onion and seeds in medium bowl. Add combined sauce, mirin, sugar and oil; toss gently to combine.

serves 4
preparation time 20 minutes
cooking time 15 minutes
nutritional count per serving 18.4g total fat (6.8g saturated fat); 1467kJ (351 cal); 7.7g carbohydrate; 35g protein; 3.7g fibre
tip If using bamboo skewers, soak them in water for at least an hour before using, to avoid splintering and scorching during cooking.

dukkah-crusted cutlets with roasted garlic yogurt

An Egyptian blend of nuts, spices and seeds, dukkah is used as a dip, when mixed with oil or into mayonnaise, or sprinkled over meats, salads or vegetables as a flavour-enhancer. Dukkah is also available, ready-made, from delicatessens and specialty spice shops.

6 cloves garlic, unpeeled
1 teaspoon vegetable oil
1 cup (280g) yogurt
12 french-trimmed
   lamb cutlets (600g)
dukkah
2 tablespoons roasted hazelnuts
2 tablespoons roasted
   pistachios
2 tablespoons sesame seeds
2 tablespoons ground coriander
1 tablespoon ground cumin

1 Preheat oven to 180°C/160°C fan-forced.
2 Place garlic on oven tray; drizzle with oil. Roast 10 minutes. Peel garlic then crush in small bowl with yogurt. Cover; refrigerate.
3 Meanwhile, make dukkah.
4 Place lamb in bowl with dukkah; turn to coat in mixture.
5 Cook lamb in heated oiled grill pan (or grill or barbecue) until cooked. Serve lamb with roasted garlic yogurt.

dukkah Blend or process nuts until chopped finely. Dry-fry seeds and spices in small frying pan until fragrant; combine with nuts in medium bowl.

serves 4
preparation time 10 minutes
cooking time 20 minutes
nutritional count per serving 27.8g total fat (8.7g saturated fat); 1547kJ (370 cal); 5.7g carbohydrate; 22.9g protein; 2.9g fibre

lamb chops with sun-dried tomato pesto

6 lamb chump chops (660g)
½ cup (125ml) lemon juice
½ cup (125ml) dry white wine
2 cloves garlic, crushed
sun-dried tomato pesto
1 cup (150g) drained sun-dried tomatoes
½ cup (125ml) olive oil
½ cup (80g) pine nuts, roasted
⅓ cup (25g) grated parmesan cheese
2 tablespoons lemon juice
2 cloves garlic, crushed

1 Trim fat from lamb. Place lamb in shallow dish; pour over combined juice, wine and garlic. Cover; refrigerate 3 hours or overnight.
2 Drain lamb; discard marinade.
3 Cook lamb on heated oiled barbecue (or grill or grill pan), uncovered, until browned and cooked as desired.
4 Meanwhile, make sun-dried tomato pesto. Serve lamb with pesto.
sun-dried tomato pesto Blend or process ingredients until combined.

serves 6
preparation time 15 minutes (plus refrigeration time)
cooking time 15 minutes
nutritional count per serving 41g total fat (8.7g saturated fat); 2182kJ (522 cal); 10.1g carbohydrate; 23.5g protein; 4.6g fibre

merguez with parmesan polenta triangles

A spicy lamb sausage that is identified by its uncooked chilli-red colour, merguez originated in Tunisia, and has become traditional fare throughout North Africa and Spain.

1 litre (4 cups) water
1 cup (170g) polenta
20g cold butter, chopped
1 cup (80g) finely grated
   parmesan cheese
8 merguez sausages (640g)
summer salad
1 small red onion (100g),
   chopped finely
4 green onions, sliced thinly
1 lebanese cucumber (130g),
   seeded, chopped finely
1 trimmed celery stalk (100g),
   sliced thinly
1 medium yellow capsicum
   (200g), chopped finely
½ cup loosely packed fresh
   flat-leaf parsley
½ cup loosely packed fresh
   mint leaves
2 teaspoons finely grated
   lemon rind
2 tablespoons lemon juice
2 tablespoons olive oil
1 tablespoon
   white wine vinegar

1 Oil deep 19cm-square cake pan.
2 Place the water in large saucepan; bring to the boil. Gradually stir polenta into water; simmer, stirring, about 10 minutes or until polenta thickens. Stir in butter and cheese. Spread polenta into pan; cool 10 minutes. Cover; refrigerate 3 hours or until firm.
3 Meanwhile, make summer salad.
4 Turn polenta onto board. Cut polenta into four squares; cut squares into triangles. Cook polenta, both sides, in heated oiled grill pan until browned and heated through. Cover to keep warm.
5 Cook sausages in same grill pan until cooked. Serve with salad and polenta.
summer salad Combine onions, cucumber, celery, capsicum and herbs in large bowl. Drizzle with combined rind, juice, oil and vinegar; toss gently.

serves 4
preparation time 25 minutes
(plus refrigeration time)
cooking time 35 minutes
nutritional count per serving 66.8g total fat
(25.7g saturated fat); 3975kJ (951 cal);
38.3g carbohydrate; 44g protein; 4.4g fibre

garlic and rosemary smoked lamb

You need 250g smoking chips for this recipe.

1kg boned rolled lamb loin
4 cloves garlic, halved
8 fresh rosemary sprigs
1 teaspoon dried chilli flakes
1 tablespoon olive oil

1 Place lamb in large shallow baking dish. Pierce lamb in eight places with sharp knife; push garlic and rosemary into cuts. Sprinkle lamb with chilli; rub with oil. Cover; refrigerate 3 hours or overnight.
2 Soak smoking chips in large bowl of water 2 hours; drain.
3 Cook lamb on heated oiled barbecue, uncovered, until browned all over.
4 Place drained smoking chips in smoke box on barbecue next to lamb. Cook lamb in covered barbecue, using indirect heat, following manufacturer's instructions, about 40 minutes or until cooked as desired.

serves 6
preparation time 10 minutes (plus refrigeration time)
cooking time 45 minutes
nutritional count per serving 17.8g total fat (7.1g saturated fat); 1254kJ (300 cal); 0.2g carbohydrate; 35g protein; 0.3g fibre
tip Smoking chips and a smoke box are available from barbecue specialty shops.

salt-rubbed roasted pork loin with sage

10 fresh sage leaves
1kg rolled pork loin (crackling and fat removed)
2 tablespoons sea salt
2 tablespoons crushed dried green peppercorns
2 tablespoons coarsely chopped fresh sage
1 tablespoon olive oil

1   Lay sage leaves in the middle of pork loin; roll pork to enclose leaves.
Tie pork at 10cm intervals with kitchen string.
2   Combine salt, peppercorns and chopped sage in small bowl.
3   Brush pork with oil; rub salt mixture over pork.
4   Place pork in disposable baking dish. Cook pork in covered barbecue,
using indirect heat, following manufacturer's instructions, about 1 hour or
until cooked through.
5   Cover with foil; stand 10 minutes before slicing.

serves 6
preparation time 15 minutes
cooking time 1 hour
nutritional count per serving 9.4g total fat (2.8g saturated fat);
974kJ (233 cal); 0.6g carbohydrate; 35.7g protein; 0.6g fibre

american-style pork spare ribs

1.5kg american-style pork spare ribs
1 cup (250ml) tomato juice
2 teaspoons grated lime rind
¼ cup (60ml) lime juice
2 tablespoons brown sugar
1 clove garlic, crushed
1 fresh small red thai chilli, chopped finely

1 Cut rib racks into individual ribs.
2 Combine remaining ingredients in large bowl; add ribs, toss to coat in marinade. Cover; refrigerate 3 hours or overnight.
3 Drain ribs; discard marinade.
4 Cook ribs in heated oiled grill pan (or grill or barbecue), uncovered, until browned and cooked through.

serves 4
preparation time 15 minutes (plus refrigeration time)
cooking time 10 minutes
nutritional count per serving 13.6g total fat (4.6g saturated fat); 1275kJ (305 cal); 8.9g carbohydrate; 36.4g protein; 0.4g fibre

glazed pork cutlets with celeriac salad

2 teaspoons honey
1 teaspoon dijon mustard
1 tablespoon olive oil
4 pork cutlets (1kg)
400g baby carrots, trimmed
celeriac salad
650g celeriac, grated coarsely
⅓ cup (100g) mayonnaise
1 clove garlic, crushed
⅓ cup (80g) light sour cream
2 tablespoons lemon juice
½ cup coarsely chopped fresh flat-leaf parsley
2 teaspoons dijon mustard

1 Whisk honey, mustard and oil in large bowl; add pork, toss to coat in mixture. Cook pork on heated oiled grill plate (or grill or barbecue) until cooked through. Cover pork; stand 5 minutes.
2 Meanwhile, boil, steam or microwave carrots until just tender; drain. Cover to keep warm.
3 Make celeriac salad.
4 Serve pork with carrots and celeriac salad.
celeriac salad Combine ingredients in medium bowl.

serves 4
preparation time 10 minutes
cooking time 15 minutes
nutritional count per serving 37.8g total fat (9.6g saturated fat); 2441kJ (584 cal); 15.5g carbohydrate; 45.6g protein; 9g fibre

barbecued vegetables and haloumi with lemon basil dressing

150g baby spinach leaves
200g char-grilled red capsicum, sliced thinly
250g grilled artichokes, halved
½ cup (60g) green olives
8 portobello mushrooms (400g)
400g haloumi cheese, sliced thickly
lemon basil dressing
2 tablespoons lemon juice
⅓ cup (80ml) olive oil
1 clove garlic, crushed
2 tablespoons finely shredded fresh basil

1 Make lemon basil dressing.
2 Combine spinach, capsicum, artichoke and olives in large bowl.
3 Cook mushrooms on heated oiled grill plate (or grill or barbecue), loosely covered with foil, about 5 minutes or until browned and tender; cover to keep warm.
4 Cook cheese over high heat on oiled grill plate until browned lightly both sides.
5 Top spinach mixture with mushrooms, cheese and dressing.
lemon basil dressing Place ingredients in screw-top jar; shake well.

serves 4
preparation time 10 minutes
cooking time 10 minutes
nutritional count per serving 40.9g total fat (14.2g saturated fat); 2224kJ (532 cal); 11.6g carbohydrate; 27.8g protein; 3.9g fibre

vegetable and tofu skewers

200g swiss brown mushrooms

1 medium green capsicum
(200g), chopped coarsely

1 medium red capsicum
(200g), chopped coarsely

1 medium yellow capsicum
(200g), chopped coarsely

3 baby eggplants (180g),
chopped coarsely

350g piece firm tofu, diced
into 3cm pieces

8 yellow patty-pan squash
(240g), halved

100g baby rocket leaves

blue cheese dressing

50g blue cheese

2 tablespoons buttermilk

200g low-fat yogurt

1 small white onion (80g),
grated finely

1 clove garlic, crushed

1 tablespoon finely chopped
fresh chives

1 tablespoon lemon juice

1 Thread mushrooms, capsicums, eggplant, tofu and squash, alternately, onto 12 skewers.

2 Cook skewers on heated oiled grill plate (or grill or barbecue) until tofu is browned all over and vegetables are just tender.

3 Meanwhile, make blue cheese dressing.

4 Serve skewers with rocket; drizzle with blue cheese dressing.

blue cheese dressing Crumble cheese into small bowl; stir in remaining ingredients.

serves 4
preparation time 10 minutes
cooking time 25 minutes
nutritional count per serving 11.1g total fat (3.7g saturated fat); 1091kJ (261 cal); 13.6g carbohydrate; 22.8g protein; 7g fibre
tip If using bamboo skewers, soak them in water for at least an hour before using, to avoid splintering and scorching during cooking.

char-grilled mediterranean vegetables in fresh oregano dressing

1 medium red capsicum (200g)

1 medium yellow capsicum (200g)

1 large red onion (300g), halved, cut into wedges

1 small kumara (250g), sliced thinly lengthways

2 baby eggplants (120g), sliced thinly lengthways

2 medium zucchini (240g), halved lengthways

340g jar artichoke hearts, drained, halved

100g seeded kalamata olives

1 small radicchio (150g), trimmed, leaves separated

fresh oregano dressing

¼ cup (60ml) olive oil

2 tablespoons red wine vinegar

2 tablespoons lemon juice

2 cloves garlic, crushed

1 tablespoon finely chopped fresh oregano

1 Make fresh oregano dressing.

2 Quarter capsicums, remove and discard seeds and membranes; cut capsicum into thick strips.

3 Cook capsicum, in batches, on heated oiled grill plate (or grill or barbecue) until browned and tender. Cook onion, kumara, eggplant, zucchini and artichoke, in batches, on grill plate until browned.

4 Combine char-grilled vegetables, olives and dressing in large bowl; toss gently. Serve with radicchio.

fresh oregano dressing Combine ingredients in screw-top jar; shake well.

serves 4
preparation time 20 minutes
cooking time 35 minutes
nutritional count per serving 14.8g total fat (2g saturated fat); 1104kJ (264 cal); 22.8g carbohydrate; 6.4g protein; 7.6g fibre
tip This salad can be made ahead with great success: the flavours of the dressing's fresh oregano and lemon will permeate the grilled vegetables and make them even more delicious.

glossary

basil an aromatic herb; there are many types, but the most commonly used is sweet, or common, basil.

bean sprouts also known as bean shoots; tender new growths of assorted beans and seeds germinated for consumption as sprouts.

blue-eye fillets also known as deep sea trevalla or trevally and blue-eye cod; thick, moist white-fleshed fish.

bread
lavash a flat, unleavened bread of Mediterranean origin.
turkish also known as pide; comes in long (about 45cm) flat loaves as well as individual rounds.

breadcrumbs stale one- or two-day-old bread made into crumbs by blending or processing.

butter use salted or unsalted (sweet) butter; 125g is equal to one stick (4 ounces) of butter.

buttermilk sold alongside fresh milk in supermarkets; despite the implication of its name, it is low in fat.

capers the grey-green buds of a warm climate (usually Mediterranean) shrub; sold dried and salted, or pickled in a vinegar brine. Rinse well before using.

capsicum also known as bell pepper or pepper. Discard seeds and membranes before use.

cardamom purchased in pod, seed or ground form. Has a distinctive aromatic, sweetly rich flavour.

celeriac tuberous root with brown skin, white flesh and a celery-like flavour.

cheese
blue mould-treated cheeses mottled with blue veining.
haloumi a firm, cream-coloured sheep-milk cheese; somewhat like a minty, salty fetta in flavour.
parmesan also known as parmigiano; a hard, grainy cow-milk cheese.

chickpeas also called garbanzos, hummus or channa; an irregularly round, sandy-coloured legume.

chilli
flakes dried, deep-red, dehydrated chilli slices and whole seeds.
powder the Asian variety, made from dried ground thai chillies, is the hottest.
thai red small, hot, and bright red in colour.

cinnamon dried inner bark of the shoots of the cinnamon tree; available in stick (quill) or ground form.

coriander also known as pak chee, cilantro or chinese parsley; bright-green leafy herb with a pungent flavour. Coriander seeds are also available but are no substitute for fresh coriander as the taste is very different.

cumin also known as zeera or comino; has a spicy, nutty flavour. Available ground or in seed form.

eggplant also known as aubergine.

fennel also known as finocchio or anise. Also the name given to dried seeds having a licorice flavour.

four-bean mix a mix of chickpeas and kidney, butter and cannellini beans.

ginger also known as green or root ginger; the thick root of a tropical plant.

hazelnuts also known as filberts.

hummus a Middle-Eastern dip made from chickpeas, garlic, lemon juice and tahini (sesame seed paste); available from delicatessens and supermarkets.

kaffir lime leaves also known as bai magrood; look like two glossy dark green leaves joined end to end, forming an hourglass shape. A strip of fresh lime peel may be substituted for each kaffir lime leaf.

kipfler potatoes small, finger-shaped potatoes having a nutty flavour.

kumara Polynesian name of orange-fleshed sweet potato often confused with yam.

lebanese cucumber short, slender and thin-skinned. Has tender, edible skin, tiny, yielding seeds and a sweet, fresh and flavoursome taste.

lemon grass a tall, clumping, lemon-smelling and tasting, sharp-edged grass; the white lower part of each stem is used.

mince also known as ground meat.

mirin sweet rice wine used in Japanese cooking; not to be confused with sake.

mushrooms
  flat large, flat mushrooms with a rich earthy flavour. Are sometimes misnamed field mushrooms, which are wild mushrooms.
  portobello large, dark-brown mushrooms with a full-bodied flavour.
  swiss brown also known as cremini or roman mushrooms; are light-brown mushrooms having a full-bodied flavour.

mustard
  dijon a pale brown, distinctively flavoured, fairly mild french mustard.
  wholegrain also known as seeded. A French-style coarse-grain mustard made from crushed mustard seeds and dijon-style mustard.

parsley, flat-leaf also known as continental parsley or italian parsley.

peppercorns, dried green, harvested when the berry is immature and then packed in brine or dried. Has a fresher and less pungent flavour than black or white peppercorns.

pine nuts also known as pignoli; not in fact a nut but a small, cream-coloured kernel from pine cones.

pistachio pale green, delicately flavoured nut inside hard off-white shells.

polenta a flour-like cereal made of ground corn (maize). Also the name of the dish made from it.

radicchio burgundy-leaved lettuce with white ribs and a slightly bitter flavour.

rice wine cooking rice wine is rice wine with salt added; sherry can be substituted.

rocket also known as rugula, arugula and rucola; a peppery-tasting green leaf.

salted black beans black soy beans that have been salted, spiced and fermented; chop or crush lightly before using.

sambal oelek (also ulek or olek); Indonesian in origin. A salty paste made from ground chillies and vinegar.

sauces
  fish also called nam pla or nuoc nam; made from salted fermented anchovies. Has a pungent smell and strong taste, so use sparingly.
  japanese soy an all-purpose low-sodium soy sauce. The best table soy and the one to choose if you only want one variety.
  sweet chilli a mild sauce made from red chillies, sugar, garlic and vinegar.

spinach also known as english spinach and, incorrectly, silver beet.

sugar
  caster also known as finely granulated or superfine table sugar.
  palm also known as jaggery or gula melaka; made from the sap of the sugar palm tree. Light-brown to dark-brown in colour and usually sold in rock-hard cakes; substitute with brown sugar.
  white coarse, granulated table sugar, also known as crystal sugar.

sumac a purple-red spice ground from berries growing on shrubs that flourish wild around the Mediterranean; adds a tart, lemony flavour.

taco seasoning mix found in most supermarkets; contains oregano, cumin, chillies and other spices.

tahini a sesame-seed paste.

vinegar
  cider (apple cider) made from fermented apples.
  red wine based on fermented red wine.
  white wine made from white wine.

witlof also known as chicory or belgian endive.

za'atar a blend of roasted spices, usually thyme, wild marjoram, sesame seeds and sumac; available from Middle-Eastern food stores.

zucchini also known as courgette.

conversion chart

MEASURES

One Australian metric measuring cup holds approximately 250ml, one Australian metric tablespoon holds 20ml, one Australian metric teaspoon holds 5ml.

The difference between one country's measuring cups and another's is within a 2- or 3-teaspoon variance, and will not affect your cooking results. North America, New Zealand and the United Kingdom use a 15ml tablespoon. All cup and spoon measurements are level. The most accurate way of measuring dry ingredients is to weigh them. When measuring liquids, use a clear glass or plastic jug with metric markings.

We use large eggs with an average weight of 60g.

DRY MEASURES

METRIC	IMPERIAL
15g	½oz
30g	1oz
60g	2oz
90g	3oz
125g	4oz (¼lb)
155g	5oz
185g	6oz
220g	7oz
250g	8oz (½lb)
280g	9oz
315g	10oz
345g	11oz
375g	12oz (¾lb)
410g	13oz
440g	14oz
470g	15oz
500g	16oz (1lb)
750g	24oz (1½lb)
1kg	32oz (2lb)

LIQUID MEASURES

METRIC	IMPERIAL
30ml	1 fluid oz
60ml	2 fluid oz
100ml	3 fluid oz
125ml	4 fluid oz
150ml	5 fluid oz (¼ pint/1 gill)
190ml	6 fluid oz
250ml	8 fluid oz
300ml	10 fluid oz (½ pint)
500ml	16 fluid oz
600ml	20 fluid oz (1 pint)
1000ml (1 litre)	1¾ pints

LENGTH MEASURES

METRIC	IMPERIAL
3mm	⅛in
6mm	¼in
1cm	½in
2cm	¾in
2.5cm	1in
5cm	2in
6cm	2½in
8cm	3in
10cm	4in
13cm	5in
15cm	6in
18cm	7in
20cm	8in
23cm	9in
25cm	10in
28cm	11in
30cm	12in (1ft)

OVEN TEMPERATURES

These oven temperatures are only a guide for conventional ovens.
For fan-forced ovens, check the manufacturer's manual.

	°C (CELSIUS)	°F (FAHRENHEIT)	GAS MARK
Very slow	120	250	½
Slow	150	275 – 300	1 – 2
Moderately slow	160	325	3
Moderate	180	350 – 375	4 – 5
Moderately hot	200	400	6
Hot	220	425 – 450	7 – 8
Very hot	240	475	9

index

ACP BOOKS
General manager Christine Whiston
Editor-in-chief Susan Tomnay
Creative director Hieu Chi Nguyen
Art director & designer Hannah Blackmore
Senior editor Wendy Bryant
Food director Pamela Clark
Food editor Louise Patniotis
Nutritional information Belinda Farlow
Sales & rights director Brian Cearnes
Marketing manager Bridget Cody
Senior business analyst Rebecca Varela
Circulation manager Jarna Mclean
Operations manager David Scotto
Production manager Victoria Jefferys

ACP Books are published by ACP Magazines
a division of PBL Media Pty Limited
PBL Media, Chief Executive Officer Ian Law
Publishing & sales director, Women's lifestyle Lynette Phillips
Group editorial director, Women's lifestyle Pat Ingram
Marketing director, Women's lifestyle Matthew Dominello
Commercial manager, Women's lifestyle Seymour Cohen
Research director, Women's lifestyle Justin Stone

Cover Veal cutlets with green olive salsa and
barbecue kipflers, page 32
Photographer Brett Stevens
Stylist David Morgan
Food preparation Angela Muscat

Back cover at left, Piri piri chicken thigh fillers, page 20;
at right, Dukkah-crusted cutlets with roasted
garlic yogurt, page 40.

Produced by ACP Books, Sydney.
Published by ACP Books,
a division of ACP Magazines Ltd,
54 Park St, Sydney; GPO Box 4088,
Sydney, NSW 2001
phone (02) 9282 8618 fax (02) 9267 9438.
acpbooks@acpmagazines.com.au
www.acpbooks.com.au
Printed by Dai Nippon in Korea.
Australia Distributed by Network Services,
phone +61 2 9282 8777; fax +61 2 9264 3278
networkweb@networkservicescompany.com.au
United Kingdom Distributed by Australian
Consolidated Press (UK),
phone (01604) 642 200; fax (01604) 642 300
books@acpuk.com
New Zealand Distributed by Netlink Distribution
Company, phone (9) 366 9966 ask@ndc.co.nz
South Africa Distributed by PSD Promotions,
phone (27 11) 392 6065/6/7; fax (27 11) 392
6079/80 orders@psdprom.co.za
Canada Distributed by Publishers Group Canada,
phone (800) 663 5714; fax (008) 565 3770;
service@raincoast.com

Grills and barbecues:
the Australian Women's Weekly.
Includes index.
ISBN 978-1-86396-733-4 (pbk).
1. Barbecue cookery. I. Clark, Pamela.
II Title: Australian Women's Weekly
641.76

Send recipe enquiries to:
recipeenquiries@acpmagazines.com.au